# Don't Pet a Pooch
## ...*While He's Pooping*

Etiquette for Dogs and Their People

# Don't Pet a Pooch
## ...*While He's Pooping*

Etiquette for Dogs
and Their People

BY **Jennifer Quasha**

ILLUSTRATIONS BY **Mary Lynn Blasutta**

Irvine, California

Karla Austin, Business Operations Manager
Jen Dorsey, Associate Editor
Michelle Martinez, Editor
Rebekah Bryant, Editorial Assistant
Ruth Strother, Editor-at-Large
Nick Clemente, Special Consultant
Vicky Vaughn, Book Designer

The dogs in this book are referred to as *he* and *she* in alternating chapters.

Library of Congress Control Number: 2004101938
ISBN 1-931993-46-7

BowTie® Press
A Division of BowTie Inc.
3 Burroughs
Irvine, California 92618

Printed and Bound in Singapore
10 9 8 7 6 5 4 3 2 1

# Dedication

For Fluffy,
une grande dame
*—Jennifer*

For all of my four-legged friends throughout the years—
Toby, Dolly, Baron Alpine, Amigo, and Tito.
*—Mary Lynn*

# Contents

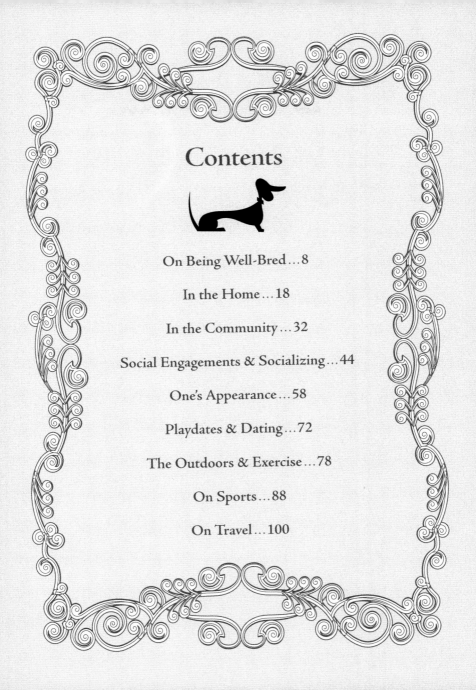

# On Being Well-Bred

## Rule One

A young dog must be
taught from an early age to
respect the mailman.

# Rule Two

 Do not inquire about *how* a dog lost his leg, eye, etc.

Just avert your gaze.

## Rule Three

Bad reputations are like mange—
difficult to get rid of.

## Rule Four

Even when in a hurry, be charitable.
Take a few seconds to allow the aged and
others to admire you.

### Rule Five

Never talk down to a dog.
Foster self-esteem by being
supportive.

## Rule Six

A dog should be considerate of all who
serve him—including the help.

# Rule Seven

A table scrap is a privilege, not a right.

## Rule Twelve

Bark only when barked at.

## Rule Thirteen

If distressed, find dirty laundry.


## Rule Fourteen

Never bark out of turn.

# Rule Fifteen

Don't let yourself be dressed up as Santa's elf
unless there's eggnog in it for you.

## Rule Sixteen

Be mindful of a lady's privates.

## Rule Seventeen

It is a sleeping dog's duty to lie.

## Rule Eighteen

A doggy bag has your name on it.

## Rule Nineteen

Puppies must be taught
not to relieve themselves on
today's newspaper.

## Rule Twenty

If confronted by a closed door,
scratch once. If unanswered,
scratch harder and faster.

## Rule Twenty-one

If your dog bed isn't goose down,
sleep on theirs.

# Rule Twenty-two

 Clean and pull whiskers in place
before going down to dinner.

# Rule Twenty-three

Reserve peeing indoors for
desperate situations.

## Rule Twenty-four

Copulation should be confined to the
bedroom, bathroom, living room, study,
playroom, kitchen, dining area, second
bedroom, garage, third bedroom, servant
quarters, attic, basement, and any other area
of your house or yard not mentioned above.

## Rule Twenty-five

Don't take family for granted.
If a member is in distress, sit
calmly and allow yourself
to be pet.

# In the Community

## Rule Twenty-six

Respect diversity.
Never bark at a person who
looks different.

## Rule Twenty-seven

Keep leashes taut and out
of the way of public
thoroughfare.

## Rule Twenty-eight

Don't lick privates in public.

### Rule Twenty-nine

When walking, if you see an obese dog,

slow down before passing.

No need to point out his handicap.

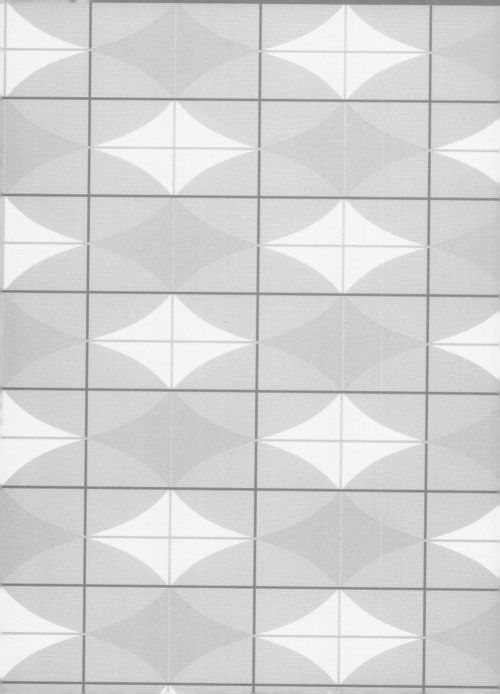

## Rule Thirty

Avoid entwined leashes when sniffing,
"Hello."

## Rule Thirty-one

If a friend gets herself knocked up,
best not to invite her to the Planning
Parenthood charity gala.

# Rule Thirty-two

Business should be done quickly,
quietly, and out of sight.

## Rule Thirty-three

Keep personal hygiene behind
closed doors. Never  scoot and
scratch on sidewalks
or in public
greens.

## Rule Thirty-four

Give an older dog the right of way.

## Rule Thirty-five

Don't pet a pooch while
he's pooping.

## Rule Thirty-six

Mentor a junkyard dog.

## Rule Thirty-seven

Stay alert! Avoid peeing on a
street person's property.

# Rule Thirty-eight

A treat offered by a stranger is
acceptable—only if it's high quality.

## Rule Thirty-nine

Well-bred dogs always use the curb.

## Rule Forty

A good neighbor is one who does not

poop on your property.

# Social Engagements
# & Socializing

## Rule Forty-one

Come up carefully from behind. No
need to startle.

### Rule Forty-two

Encourage extracurricular activities.
Take your dog to birthday parties, playdates, etc.

### Rule Forty-three

Be courteous. Arrive to social
engagements promptly.

### Rule Forty-four

Invite the ugly dogs to your parties.
It will mean so much.

## Rule Forty-five

Be involved in your community.
Visit elderly, donate gently used
leashes, etc.

## Rule Forty-six

If complimented, pay one in
return. If necessary, be quick in
making one up.

# Rule Forty-seven

 Welcome new dogs to your
community by baking treats.

### Rule Forty-eight

Acknowledge compliments

with a demure wag.

## Rule Forty-nine

On St. Francis Day, don't cut in line—
even if you have to wait behind rodents,
iguanas, etc.

## Rule Fifty

Always give friends the benefit of the doubt.

Unless you find him in your treat bag,

mounting your bitch, etc.

## Rule Fifty-one

If you suddenly don't remember a dog,

bluff your way by eager wagging.

# Rule Fifty-two

Under no circumstance should you enter into
muttrimony lightly—including same sex unions.

## Rule Fifty-three

If something smells foul, wait until others are
occupied before investigating.

## Rule Fifty-four

Don't discriminate against a breed.
Who knows who the creature's
friends are.

## Rule Fifty-five

If a person says something inappropriate
in the dog run, wag your tail vaguely
and move away.

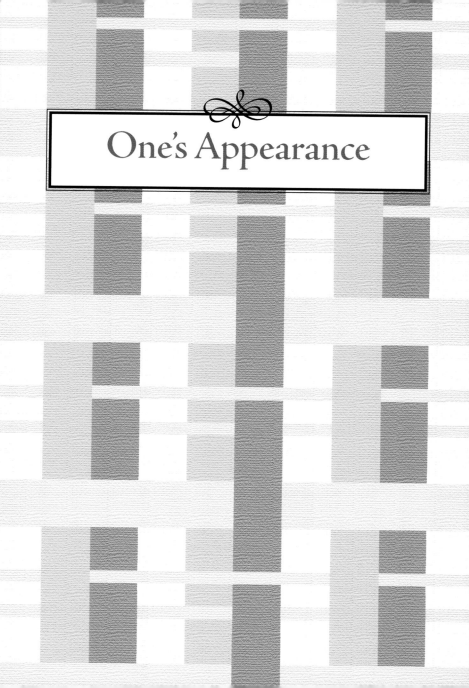

# One's Appearance

## Rule Fifty-six

Clothing should never be too loose or
too tight. Chose well-tailored clothes
to suit and enhance the figure.

# Rule Fifty-seven

A Halloween costume is actually a chew toy.

### Rule Fifty-eight

Keep nails short. Avoid clicking noises
across hardwood floors.

### Rule Fifty-nine

Always encourage your dog's natural look.
Leave boas to constrictors.

## Rule Sixty

It's preferable to have fewer
items but of the highest quality
you can afford.

## Rule Sixty-one

If you need a new collar-leash ensemble
for an event, never wait until the last
minute to shop. You won't end up with
the most enhancing option.

### Rule Sixty-two

It's imperative to read *Dog Fancy*, *Dog World*, and
other respected publications to stay on top of
current events and the world at large.

### Rule Sixty-three

When rising from a seated position, pooches
must remember to keep their legs together.

### Rule Sixty-four

When accessorizing, do not overdo.
Before you leave home take one accessory off.

## Rule Sixty-five

Studs who drool must carry

handkerchiefs.

## Rule Sixty-six

Under no circumstance must a dog wear
fur that is not his own.

### Rule Sixty-seven

When overheated, don't pant
directly into someone else's
mug. You might kill him.

# Rule Sixty-eight

 Posture is crucial to a positive outward appearance.

When seated, rump should be balanced and firmly planted. Front and hind legs ought to run parallel to one another. Nose should be raised and jaw line perpendicular to the floor. Be careful not to overextend either nose or neck.

When standing, shoulders and hips should rest high upon legs. All paws ought to face forward. Muscles should be engaged, but not overwrought.

### Rule Sixty-nine

Keep nails trimmed and hair brushed.
Anything other demonstrates bad pedigree.

### Rule Seventy

No white paws after Labor Day.

# Playdates & Dating

### Rule Seventy-one

Discourage your dog from playdating
with mangy bitches.

## Rule Seventy-two

It is not appropriate for puppies under
three months of age to playdate.


## Rule Seventy-three

Encourage your dog to play with
his current playdate even if a cuter
bitch comes along.

## Rule Seventy-four

Make an effort to find something
nice to say to a dog who has
endured a bad groom.

## Rule Seventy-five

A bitch in heat must
be chaperoned.

## Rule Seventy-six

Always let your bitch through the
doggy door first.

# The Outdoors & Exercise

## Rule Seventy-seven

Exercise is best when you
are in the arms of a person
who is doing the running.

# Rule Seventy-eight

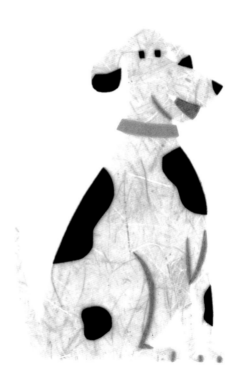

Never catch a dirty tennis ball. You never know whose mouth touched it last.

## Rule Seventy-nine

When playing fetch let the fat dog
get it once in a while.

## Rule Eighty

Never let them strap a backpack to you
when hiking. If you have to sleep in the
woods, they should carry your goods.

# Rule Eighty-one

Only a daft dog chases a cat

with claws.

## Rule Eighty-two

The only way to truly enjoy the outdoors
is by rolling in something dead.

# Rule Eighty-three

Chasing squirrels is fruitless.

Be a dog of leisure.

## Rule Eighty-four

If they force you to go out in the rain,
shake dry on the Oriental rug. Muddy
paws on white carpet works too.

### Rule Eighty-five

At the beach, remember—
sand-free towels are meant
to be tread upon.

### Rule Eighty-six

A child's beach shovel
makes a great chew toy.
Plus it floats.

### Rule Eighty-seven

Never drink seawater.
A bottle of Evian is
never far.

# On Sports

## Rule Eighty-eight

Only white dogs, or dogs in white attire,
are allowed on the croquet court.

# Rule Eighty-nine

When cruising on a yacht, wear a life preserver—even a capable water dog could fall overboard and drown if hit by the boom.

### Rule Ninety

Always listen to the
captain's orders—if you
agree with them.

### Rule Ninety-one

When walking the golf
course, avoid barking—
even at squirrels. It distracts
club members.

## Rule Ninety-two

Help replace divots—but do not take the
blame for digging them.

## Rule Ninety-three

Always ride in the front of the golf cart to
help sniff for wayward shots.

## Rule Ninety-four

All dogs must wear a collar
on the golf course.

# Rule Ninety-five

Do not move a lying ball.

Even if no one can see you.

## Rule Ninety-six

Dogs with long nails are prohibited
from walking on the greens.

## Rule Ninety-seven

Peeing in cups is prohibited.

## Rule Ninety-eight

Paw prints in bunkers
are not tolerated.

## Rule Ninety-nine

Tennis spectators must not be
distracting—even if you have your
eyes on the ball.

# On Travel

## Rule One hundred

Keep travel documents up-to-date.
There are no home-cooked meals
in quarantine.

# Rule One hundred and one

Pack smart. Remember to bring:

Wet food

Dry food

Semi-wet food

Semi-dry food

Chicken-flavored rawhide

Beef-flavored rawhide

Plain rawhide (in case of illness)

Pig's ears

Collars:

    Leather and/or rhinestone collar for evenings

    Ribbon collar for daytime

    Nylon collar for working out

Matching leashes for above collars

Treats, treats, and treats

Low-fat treats (before bed)

Full-fat treats (middle of the night)

Squeaky hamburger

Fetch toy (if you fetch)

Chew toy (warm up for hotel drapes)

Chicken-flavored toothpaste

Toothbrush (if you brush, which you should)

### Rule One hundred and two

You never know if travel plans will go awry.

Pack an extra two days of treats.

## Rule One hundred and three

Only chew drapes if left alone
in the suite.

## Rule One hundred and four

Pet friendly establishments are okay.
The Four Seasons and the Ritz are grand.

# Rule One hundred and five

Pack heavy items first, and take care to put treats on top for easy access.

## Rule One hundred and six

If possible, go on a cruise—there are
endless droppings from overweight
passenger's plates.

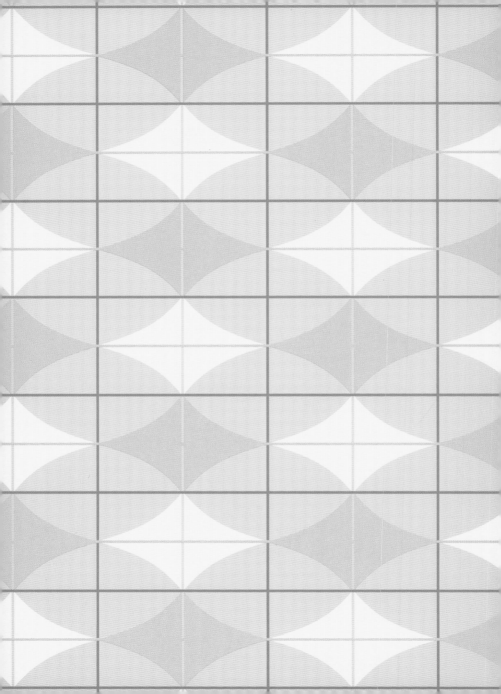

### Rule One hundred and seven
Avoid traveling via commercial air.
Find friends with jets.

### Rule One hundred and eight
If you must travel by commercial
plane, yap continuously when
stowed under the seat.

### Rule One hundred and nine
Ask for Chicken *and* Beef.

# Rule One hundred and ten

An open window of a racing automobile
provides a superior nose rush—be sure to
hold on tight.

## Rule One hundred and eleven

When traveling via taxi or car never lie down
on pleather or naugahyde.

### Rule One hundred and twelve

In an automobile, as in life, if left alone, wreak havoc.

Next time you won't be.